A DAY IN THE LIFE

Bears

WHAT DO POLAR BEARS, GIANT PANDAS,
AND GRIZZLY BEARS GET UP
TO ALL DAY?

NEON 🦑 SQUID

Contents

Welcome to the world of bears!

Carnivores (meat-eaters) are some of the most charismatic animals on the planet. I've been fascinated by them from the first time I watched *The Jungle Book* as a young child. As I learned more about these animals I fell in love with the world of wildlife and nature as a whole. Now I am a **wildlife biologist** and I spend my days working with a variety of species, including foxes, bats, and—of course—bears!

There are eight bear species scattered across the globem, each one unique in how it navigates the world. In my job, I spend some of my time studying black bears to understand how they interact with a landscape dominated by humans. Many bear species are **threatened or endangered**. It is important to know how humans are impacting their survival, so we can focus our conservation efforts.

Bears are **highly intelligent** creatures who have captured the hearts of people around the globe with their behavior. You might have questions about these amazing animals. Do all bears hibernate? What lengths will a mother go to protect her cubs? Is there an aquatic bear? Join me as we spend a day finding out why bears are such a fascinating group of animals. Enjoy the ride!

Don W. Hardeman Jr.

Brave new world

It's dawn in Tate's Hell, a forest in Florida. The early morning light breaks through the canopy of the cypress swamp where a mother and son share their **final moments** together.

These creatures are American black bears, but don't be fooled by the name. Not all black bears are black. They can also come in various shades of brown and even red, white, and blue!

The young bear, called a yearling, nuzzles his mother. It may seem sad to us, but it isn't just important this male leaves his mom—it's necessary. Doing so will prevent him from being killed by any **larger males** in the area that would view him as future competition for food and mates.

Armed with his mother's love and the life lessons she's taught him, the yearling sets off along a fallen tree trunk to make his way in the world.

Meanwhile... Sockeye salmon begin the long swim upstream to reach their spawning grounds. However, danger lurks ahead...

Break the ice

The sun rises on a blank white canvas in the Arctic Circle. The morning is completely silent, the snow dampening all sound, until... **CRACKKK!** A pile of snow and ice tumbles away and out pops the head of a female polar bear! She shifts her head from side to side, using her keen senses to get her bearings.

Tucked away in the den behind her are two little faces with eyes that look like black marbles stuck onto cotton wool. The cubs push against each other as they fight over who gets to leave first. It's been four months since this mother bear (a sow) started **hibernating** in her den, and two months since she gave birth. The little ones push past her, the soft snow crunching beneath their paws. They spend a few minutes tussling with each other before mom signals it's time to go. Everyone is hungry, and they need to find food if the cubs are to survive.

Protect and conserve

Today there are eight species of bear alive on the planet. As humans, it is our responsibility to protect and conserve these magnificent creatures. Let's meet the family!

Sloth bear
Location: Indian subcontinent
Status: Vulnerable

It is estimated that there are only 20,000 sloth bears left in the wild. India has passed laws to protect the species.

Spectacled bear
Location: South America
Status: Vulnerable

The only species of bear found in South America. This bear is the only surviving relative of the extinct short-faced bears.

Sun bear
Location: Southeast Asia
Status: Vulnerable

These bears mostly feed on ants, termites, beetle larvae, honey, and fruit. They are called "honey bears" in Indonesia because of their love of the sweet food!

Giant panda
Location: China
Status: Vulnerable

China and other countries have undertaken a high-profile effort to save this species. Thanks to their efforts pandas are no longer endangered, but there is still work to do to protect them.

American black bear
Location: North America
Status: Least concern

With a population of more than 900,000 individuals, the American black bear is one of only two species of bear not threatened by global extinction (the other is the brown bear).

Giant short-faced bear

Location: North America
Status: Extinct

Sadly these giant bears are no longer alive. Scientific research suggests these creatures could run at speeds of up to 40 mph (64 kph).

As well as giant short-faced bears, there were once lesser short-faced bears too.

Asiatic black bear

Location: Asia
Status: Vulnerable

These bears are threatened due to hunting and the destruction of their forest habitat by humans.

Brown bear

Location: North America, Europe, and Asia
Status: Least concern

Brown bears that live in North America are called grizzly bears. Half of all grizzlies are found in Alaska.

Polar bear

Location: The Arctic
Status: Vulnerable

Polar bears are struggling due to climate change, which has caused sea ice to melt. This has led to habitat loss and a lack of hunting opportunities.

King of the clouds

Next we journey to the Andean cloud forests of Peru, where a male spectacled bear is making his way along the forest floor. Suddenly the male, also called a boar, hears a loud noise in the distance. He starts climbing up a tree so he can find out where the sound is coming from.

Spectacled bears are **arboreal**, meaning they live in trees. This male is a skilled climber, and it isn't long before he's at the top of the tree. He steps out onto a lone branch and surveys the valley below. He listens as the familiar sounds of humans and heavy machinery fell another precious tree in the forest he calls home.

This **deforestation** is not good news for our spectacled bear. He is dependent on a healthy forest to provide him with plenty of food. Without the forest the bear may be forced to come closer to human villages and towns to search for food.

Liquid
gold

Wandering through the dense tropical forests of Southeast Asia are a female sun bear and her two yearlings. The air is **hot and steamy**, and these young bears are starting to get hungry. Just then they come across a beehive. It will make the perfect snack! But there's a problem: It's hanging from a tall branch. Sun bears are the smallest of the bear species, and the female is unable to reach the hive even standing at full height.

However, all is not lost—the two mischievous yearlings have a plan. These bears are excellent climbers, and the female yearling uses her strong forepaws to scale the tree trunk. Then she paws at the beehive until it falls on her brother. **THWACK!** The male yearling is covered in honey! He uses his extremely long tongue to slurp up as much as possible, while his mom goes about the delicious task of cleaning him up.

Meanwhile... An adult male American black bear rubs against a tree near his favorite berry patch. He's leaving his scent as a warning to any other bears who might think about trespassing!

Catch of the day

Sockeye salmon head to the ocean as youngsters and return to rivers as adults to breed.

It's breakfast time in British Columbia, a province in Canada. A female grizzly bear wades into the icy water of a river while her cubs watch from the safety of the bank. Other bears are already busy fishing nearby. **Sockeye salmon** swim and dart around her as they make their way upstream toward the spawning grounds where they will breed.

The sow carefully makes her way toward the edge of the waterfall to face the salmon at their most vulnerable: the moment they **leap up the waterfall**. She plants all four paws in the river for stability, keeps her eye on the rushing water, and waits for the right opportunity.

Suddenly a sockeye salmon leaps toward her. **SNAP!!** She grabs it in her jaws. Her two cubs watch as their mom carries her catch back to the riverbank. Breakfast is served!

11AM A very hungry family

Shunan Bamboo Sea, the largest and oldest bamboo forest, covers 27 mountain ridges and 500 hills in Southwest China. It's here we find a family of giant panda bears. Like the other bears in this book, the pandas are hungry. But unlike their cousins, pandas are **folivores**, which means they eat leaves.

The sow relies on her memory to find succulent bamboo for her yearlings to eat. Using a special thumb, she holds the bamboo steady while she plucks leaves from the stalk.

Bamboo doesn't provide much in terms of energy, so these pandas scoff down the leaves by the pawful. The yearlings will spend the day trudging through the forest as their mom teaches them where to find the **best bamboo patches**. Her yearlings will use this knowledge for years to come.

Pandas need to spend 12 to 15 hours a day eating bamboo leaves to survive!

Swiss Army knife

Bears are the ultimate survivors. Over time they have evolved different tools to suit a variety of environments and help them to thrive. They're the animal equivalent of a Swiss Army knife!

Amazing jaws

Bears are equipped with powerful jaws, capable of exerting bone-crushing force. But they can also delicately pluck a cub from the ground without hurting it. Inside their jaws are sharp teeth for tearing flesh, cracking nuts, or chewing bamboo leaves.

Tongue twister

Bears have an extremely dextrous tongue that they use kind of like we use our hands, or a monkey uses its tail. These tongues are capable of picking berries one by one!

Crafty claws

All bears are equipped with a set of sharp claws on their paws. They use them to climb trees, tear apart beehives and termite mounds, defend themselves, and hunt.

The nose knows

Bears have one of the best senses of smell in the animal kingdom. Animals use things called olfactory receptors to obtain information on each smell they encounter. Let's compare a bear's sense of smell to other great sniffers!

Wolf
280 million olfactory receptors

Grizzly bear
230 million olfactory receptors

Bloodhound
230 million olfactory receptors

Human
5 million olfactory receptors

Need for speed

Think you could beat a bear in a race? Think again! Despite their often large size, some bears can reach speeds of up to 35 mph (56 kph). That's faster than the quickest human ever!

Brainiacs

Bears are highly intelligent creatures that can solve complex problems when trying to find food. Some people install special locks on their trash cans, and the bears still manage to get in!

12PM Seal of approval

Its midday when the polar bear sow reaches her hunting grounds with her cubs in tow. This area of sea ice is where these cubs will spend most of their time. Here their mother will teach them how to hunt for seals, which provide an important, **energy-rich** source of food that is critical to their survival.

The sow stands by the water's edge. Watching. Waiting. Suddenly there is a flash of movement beneath the water's surface. It's a **harbor seal**. In an instant, the polar bear dives in. The chase is on!

The seal glides between submerged chunks of ice, hoping its speed will save it. The sow trails behind. A strong swimmer, she uses her **slightly webbed forepaws** to propel herself through the water. SWOOSH! The seal takes a wrong turn, and the polar bear grabs it in her jaws. The cubs will eat well today!

Polar bears are just as
comfortable among sea ice
as they are on land.

He's behind you...

Leaving his mom was difficult enough, but now the young American black bear faces his first challenge: surviving the day! That means finding his own food, since his mother is no longer around to help him. Black bears **mostly eat plants**, so that makes the search for food a little easier. After walking through the forest for a short while, the yearling is delighted to find a patch of ripe, tasty blueberries.

However, in his excitement to scoff down the sweet meal he misses the **large claw marks** on a nearby tree—the telltale sign that this is another bear's home...

A hulking figure lurks in the shadows behind the bear. The youngster picks up the scent of the other bear, but too late. A **colossal adult male** bursts out of the undergrowth and charges at him! These blueberries are tasty, but not worth dying for. The yearling scampers away as fast as he can!

Watch your step!

Tiny claws scrape bark as two spectacled bear cubs scurry up a tree in pursuit of their mom. While they are young these cubs require all of their mother's attention. Today's lesson: what plants in the forest can be eaten and what plants may be poisonous and are better avoided.

In their excitement, one of the cubs **loses its footing**, grabbing onto a branch at the last second to prevent itself from falling to the ground below.

The second cub cries out as its sibling's grip loosens. It won't be able to hold on for much longer! Luckily their mother has heard the cries. She delicately plucks her cub off the branch and carries it to a **safe spot** further along the tree. The tiny cub relaxes in the grip of her mouth. Female bears like this mother invest a large amount of time and energy into raising their cubs. It just goes to show—you can't leave them alone for five minutes!

Feasting on scraps

Not too far from the inland river where the grizzly bears are fishing for salmon, another group of grizzlies has found something much larger to eat...

A dead blue whale has washed ashore on a rocky Canadian beach. This is too good an opportunity to turn down and it's first come, first served! It's rare for such an event to happen, and the whale carcass quickly becomes a communal feeding ground for a group of sows of different ages. If a **large alpha male** was around he would prevent any other bears from eating the whale, but these sows are in luck.

The bears don't hold back. They hungrily tear at the flesh of the whale. Between gorging on salmon, berries, and other lucky finds like beached whales, these grizzly bears can dramatically increase their size through the late summer and fall. This period of continuous feeding is known as **hyperphagia**. It's really important that bears put on as much weight as possible during this phase. They will need all the energy they can muster for the cold winter months ahead when they might hibernate and give birth to cubs.

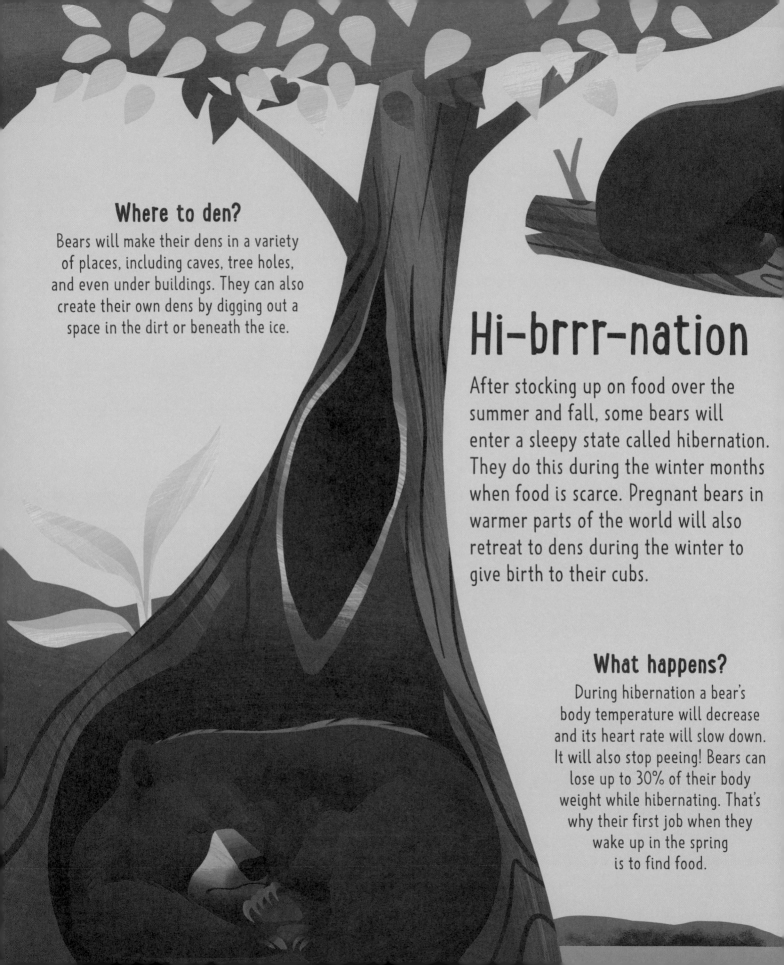

Where to den?

Bears will make their dens in a variety of places, including caves, tree holes, and even under buildings. They can also create their own dens by digging out a space in the dirt or beneath the ice.

Hi-brrr-nation

After stocking up on food over the summer and fall, some bears will enter a sleepy state called hibernation. They do this during the winter months when food is scarce. Pregnant bears in warmer parts of the world will also retreat to dens during the winter to give birth to their cubs.

What happens?

During hibernation a bear's body temperature will decrease and its heart rate will slow down. It will also stop peeing! Bears can lose up to 30% of their body weight while hibernating. That's why their first job when they wake up in the spring is to find food.

The non-hibernators

Not all bears hibernate. Those in tropical climates have plentiful food resources all year round, so they won't spend time in dens unless they're raising cubs. Spectacled bears, sun bears, sloth bears, and giant pandas live in these regions. That's half of all bear species!

Natal dens

Cubs are born and nursed in a natal den, also known as a maternal den. How long it takes for the cubs to develop depends on how much milk the sow produces and how many cubs she has to feed.

Ready, set, play!

Unlike humans, bears are usually quiet when playing.

It's mid-afternoon and our family of giant pandas are climbing higher into the mountains when tiny crystals start to fall from the sky. **It's snowing!** Luckily, panda bears don't hibernate, or the mom and her yearlings would have missed the snow day.

The two brothers are well-fed and healthy, so what do they do in the snow? They start to play of course! It isn't long before they're tumbling down a snowy hill after each other. Adult pandas don't tend to play as much as cubs, but this mom can't resist joining in. She rolls a **large snowball**.

For these yearlings, playing isn't just about fun. Scientists think play as juveniles may help brain development, improve paw coordination, and strengthen social bonds. Essentially it is a safe way for the bears to test their abilities.

Meanwhile... In the grasslands of India a female Bengal tiger picks up a scent. Thinking it could be her next meal, she decides to investigate.

Sloth bears are the most aggressive bear species.

Clash of the titans

The Bengal tiger follows the scent until, just ahead of her, she spies a sloth bear with **two cubs on her back**. Primed and ready to strike, she waits for the perfect moment... Then, in a flash of stripes, she ambushes the bears!

The startled mother sloth bear huffs and gnashes her teeth. The tigress arches her back, flattens her ears, exposes her canine teeth, and **extends her claws**.

They're also the only bears that carry their cubs on their back!

Despite being physically outmatched, the female bear stands her ground. Both of these mothers have something to fight for: The sow needs to defend her cubs. The tigress is in need of a meal to feed her cubs. The sow charges the tiger, emitting a **guttural cry**. The animals clash! With bared teeth the sow swipes at the tigress, forcing her to back up. The two mothers circle each other, waiting for the other to make a move. The tigress pounces, missing the bear's flank by mere inches. While all this is going on the cubs cling to their mother for dear life. Exhausted, the sow senses an opportunity to end the fight and charges the tigress at full force. It works! Fearing injury, the tigress turns and runs.

Snared!

Exhausted after his death-defying escape from the large male, the yearling American black bear finds himself in an unexplored part of the forest. The sun is starting to set. Starving, the bear picks up the scent of **something sweet**.

Following his nose, he stumbles upon an odd-looking contraption with an unknown smell. In the middle, balanced on a tree stump, is a pile of **delicious doughnuts**. Wary, the bear walks around the trees, keeping his eyes fixed on the sweet treats.

Snagged bear hair

Sensing no immediate threat, he climbs through the silver wire that surrounds the doughnuts. Inside, the yearling male gets to enjoy the meal without interruption.

Once he's had his fill, the yearling slides under the fence and continues on his journey to find a new home. Meanwhile, the barbed wire has served its purpose: to **snag a hair** from the yearling's back. This contraption is a snare that was placed here by a biologist to get a sample from the bear without it noticing. And it's worked!

Cage traps

This method involves enticing a bear into a trap with food. Once inside, the door slides shut so the bear can't escape. Cage traps allow biologists to safely capture bears without harming themselves or the animals.

Bear research

In order to protect bears, we need to understand them. Wildlife biologists use a variety of techniques to study bears in the wild. Which method they use depends on the question they are trying to answer and what is best for the bear.

Ear tags

Once a bear has been tranquilized scientists sometimes attach ear tags. This allows them to identify individual bears in the wild. Knowing which bear is which allows scientists to study their behavior more accurately.

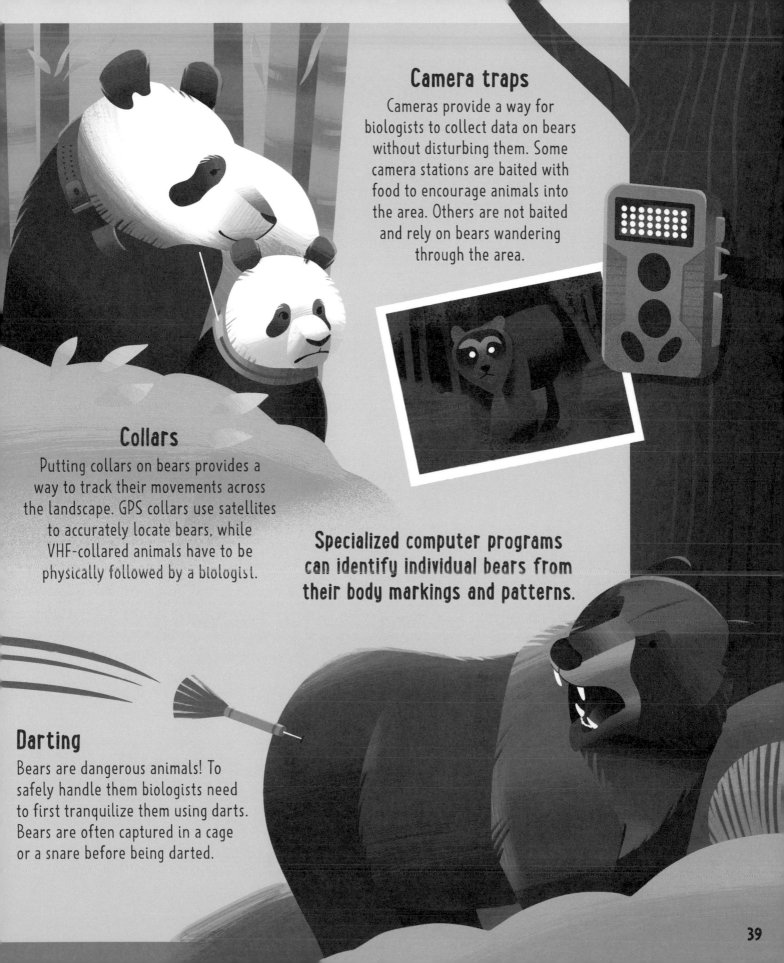

Camera traps

Cameras provide a way for biologists to collect data on bears without disturbing them. Some camera stations are baited with food to encourage animals into the area. Others are not baited and rely on bears wandering through the area.

Collars

Putting collars on bears provides a way to track their movements across the landscape. GPS collars use satellites to accurately locate bears, while VHF-collared animals have to be physically followed by a biologist.

Specialized computer programs can identify individual bears from their body markings and patterns.

Darting

Bears are dangerous animals! To safely handle them biologists need to first tranquilize them using darts. Bears are often captured in a cage or a snare before being darted.

Fight night

The green and blue colors of the aurora borealis dance in the sky as two gigantic male polar bears square off against each other. Male polar bears tend to avoid each other for most of the year, but during the **breeding season** they will compete to find a mate. And this can lead to highly aggressive behavior...

It doesn't take long before these two males—one young, one old—stand and attack each other. They bite and paw, tear and claw. The older boar has **size and power** on his side. He eventually manages to fight off the smaller male, receiving only a few minor wounds. However, he knows it's only a matter of time before a younger, stronger polar bear will take his position. After all, he did exactly the same thing many moons ago.

Male polar bears are the largest carnivores (meat-eaters) on land.

The termite eater

Fending off the tigress has left the mother sloth bear very tired, so she leaves her cubs somewhere safe and begins to forage for food. There's something in particular she is searching for. She uses her excellent sense of smell to locate the target: a **termite mound!** Sloth bears are the only species of bear that have evolved to hunt termites and ants.

A beacon in the darkness, the termite mound is unprepared for the coming threat. Using her sickle-shaped claws, the sow tears into the mound. She removes dirt with violent puffs from her mouth. **PWOOSH!**

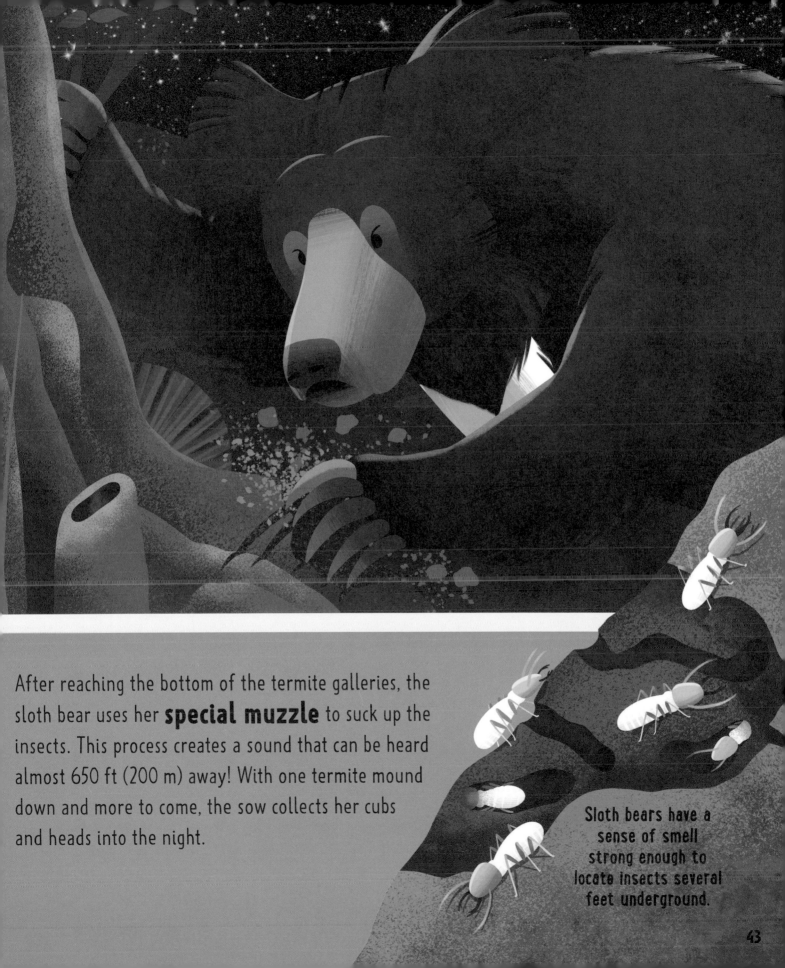

After reaching the bottom of the termite galleries, the sloth bear uses her **special muzzle** to suck up the insects. This process creates a sound that can be heard almost 650 ft (200 m) away! With one termite mound down and more to come, the sow collects her cubs and heads into the night.

Sloth bears have a sense of smell strong enough to locate insects several feet underground.

Creature of the night

Darkness covers the land as we meet our final bear. Deep in the Himalayan mountains of Tibet, an Asiatic black bear makes her way out of her den.

This **nocturnal bear** shelters during the day and forages at night. Fruit and nuts are her meal of choice, but like most bears she is omnivorous—meaning she eats meat as well as plants. The occasional insect or rodent would be welcome in her belly.

The sow makes her way down the tree, taking a moment to glance back toward her cubs. The **V-shaped crest** on her chest catches the light. It's responsible for her other name: the moon bear. She's not the only mother to say goodbye to her cubs today, but at least this separation is temporary. Before the night is out she will return to the warmth of the den.

Glossary

Alpha male
The dominant male animal in a group.

Arboreal
An animal that mainly lives in trees.

Aurora borealis
A natural light display that occurs in the Earth's northern hemisphere. Also known as the northern lights.

Boar
An adult male bear.

Carnivore
An animal that eats meat.

Climate change
The long-term change in global climate patterns often linked to the rise in global temperatures.

Deforestation
The process of removing trees from a large area so the land can be used for other purposes.

Extinct
Refers to a species of animal or plant that has died out and no longer exists on Earth.

Hibernation
The process certain species undergo where they spend the winter in a dormant (sleepy) state and are not active.

Hyperphagia
A period where animals eat excessively to put on weight to prepare for the winter months.

Natal den
The location where female bears give birth and keep their young while nursing them.

Nocturnal
An animal that is mostly active at night.

Omnivore
An animal that eats both plants and meat.

Predator
An animal that hunts and eats other animals.

Sow
An adult female bear.

Spawning grounds
The location where most aquatic animals (such as fish or frogs) go to lay their eggs.

Wildlife biologist
A scientist who studies animals in the wild.

Yearling
An animal that is one year old.

Index

This has been a

NEON 🦑 SQUID

production

To my mom: Thank you for encouraging my love of reading and passion for wildlife.

To the future wildlife biologist reading this: Mine was not always an easy journey. May the road ahead be paved with once-in-a-lifetime experiences. As you leave your mark on the wildlife profession remember these three things: Be humble. Be passionate. Extend an opportunity to those who follow in your footsteps.

Author: Don W. Hardeman Jr.
Illustrator: Rebecca Mills

Editorial Assistant: Malu Rocha
US Editor: Allison Singer Kushnir
Proofreader: Laura Gilbert

Copyright © 2023 St. Martin's Press
120 Broadway, New York, NY 10271

Created for St. Martin's Press
by Neon Squid
The Stables, 4 Crinan Street,
London, N1 9XW

EU representative: Macmillan
Publishers Ireland Ltd,
1st Floor, The Liffey Trust Centre,
117–126 Sheriff Street Upper,
Dublin 1, D01 YC43

10 9 8 7 6 5 4 3 2 1

The right of Don W. Hardeman Jr.
to be identified as the author of
this work has been asserted in
accordance with the Copyright,
Designs and Patents Act 1988.

Library of Congress Cataloging-in-
Publication Data is available.

Printed and bound in Guangdong,
China by Leo Paper Products Ltd.

ISBN: 978-1-684-49310-4

Published in September 2023.

www.neonsquidbooks.com